Speech Zero to Hero in One Hour

Create a Presentation in an Hour
that Will Wow Your Audience

Diane Windingland

Contents

Introduction

Do you need to create a presentation in a hurry, but you're feeling a little overwhelmed?

Do you want to "wow" your audience with your confidence and clarity?

Do you just want to get your presentation done?

I'm Diane Windingland, a presentation coach for subject matter experts, and I'll show you how to go from Speech Zero to Hero in One Hour.

Using this book, you can get your presentation done in about an hour if:

1. You are knowledgeable about your content.
2. You have no, or very few, presentation slides.
3. You stick to the time limits for each speech development worksheet. There are 6 speech development worksheets, plus a focused practice.

If you need to do some research, if you have slides to prepare, or if you want to devote more time to preparation and practice, it will just take longer, but the process is the same.

How to use this book:

1. You can read through this short book in a few minutes to get the approach, and set it aside, until you really need it. Or, just use a few of the ideas.

2. You can work on a presentation, either your own, or on a suggested practice presentation. A second set of worksheets is provided near the end of this book.

Your 1 Hour Timeline:

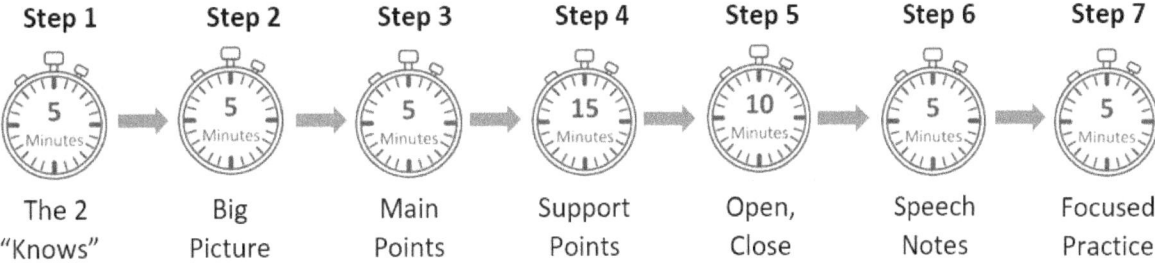

If you do the math, you'll note that the times only add up to 50 minutes. The additional 10 minutes are for reading the short introductions to each worksheet.

Step 1: The 2 Knows

Before you plunge into creating your presentation there are a couple of critical things you should know to save time and frustration later:

The first thing you should know are the requirements such as date, time, location, and length of your presentation. This may be obvious, but these are things you don't want to overlook!

The second thing to know is YOUR audience. There are a few questions to consider, but the most basic one is, "Why would the audience care about your topic?"

If you don't have a specific speech you want to work on, here are a couple of general ideas for the purposes of practicing this approach:

Practice Topics: "Life lessons." Or, "Career Lessons."

If you are using a practice topic instead of a specific presentation you need to give, you can assume that your audience is a group of students in your field of expertise.

Let's get started! You have 5 minutes to complete worksheet #1: The 2 Knows.

 # Worksheet #1: The 2 "Knows"

Speech Zero to Hero in One Hour from VirtualSpeechCoach.com

Understanding a couple of critical considerations before you start creating your presentation will save you time and frustration later!

#1 Know the Requirements

Date:
Time:
Location:
Length of presentation:
Topic:
What you are expected to bring (e.g. handout/report/introduction):

Other:

#2 Know Your Audience

Audience composition (executives, peers, customers, etc.):

Is there a segment of the audience of primary importance?

What level of knowledge about my topic does the audience have?

What are the audience pain points, as related to your topic?
  Pain point 1:
  Pain point 2:
  Pain point 3:

Why would the audience care about your topic?

What do you want the audience to think, feel, and/or do?
Think:
Feel:
Do (do you have a call-to-action?):

Step 2: The Big Picture

The big picture is knowing your purpose for the presentation and your overall approach to presenting it.

First decide on your purpose, both general and specific

General purpose—to inform, to persuade, or to entertain (possibly a combination)

Specific purpose—consider your audience analysis from worksheet #1, and then combine your general purpose with a benefit statement for your audience.

Here is an example, using the "Life Lessons" topic:

General purpose: to persuade

Specific purpose: To persuade recent engineering grads that developing public speaking skills will enhance their careers

Second, decide on an organizational structure—what makes sense for your topic?

- Topical: Most common presentation structure, arranges information into subtopics

- Binary: Problem-Solution, Cause-Effect, Compare-Contrast, Advantages-Disadvantages

- Sequential: Chronological, Demonstration (step 1, step 2, step 3)

- Spatial (parts relating to a whole, geographical)

For the example "Life Lessons" topic, I'd probably pick topical, or maybe problem-solution.

You have 5 minutes to complete worksheet #2 Big Picture

Worksheet #2: Big Picture

Speech Zero to Hero in One Hour from VirtualSpeechCoach.com

Start with your purpose and decide on your organizational structure to support that purpose.

#1 Select ONE Specific Purpose (keeping in mind your audience)

Step 1: What is the main general purpose of your presentation?
Circle one: To inform, to persuade, to entertain

Step 2: What is your specific purpose? (start your statement with your general purpose and phrase it to include a benefit for the audience)

Example: *To persuade engineers that developing public speaking skills will enhance their careers.* (the benefit is "enhance their careers")

> **Your specific purpose:**

#2 Decide on an organizational structure to communicate your main idea

- Topical: Most common presentation structure, arranges information into subtopics

- Binary: Problem-Solution, Cause-Effect, Compare-Contrast, Advantages-Disadvantages

- Sequential: Chronological, Demonstration (step 1, step 2, step 3)

- Spatial (parts relating to a whole, geographical)

> **Your presentation structure:**
>
> **Speech Title:**

Step 3: Main Points

If you are preparing to give a speech in an hour, you don't have time to figure out a lot of main points, so keep it to 2 or 3. By limiting the number of main points to 2 or 3, not only will they be easier for the audience to remember, they will be easier for you to remember, too!

Spend just a couple of minutes brainstorming at least 7 possible main points.

Ask: Does it support my purpose? Is it relevant to my audience?

Then narrow down or combine your ideas into 2-3 main points.

Here is what I chose for the example topic *(To persuade recent engineering grads that developing public speaking skills will enhance their careers)*, with points 2 and 3 being problem-solution:

1. Public speaking skills are important for engineers (topic main point)
2. Public speaking skills can be challenging for engineers (problem)
3. Opportunities to improve public speaking skills (solution)

Are you ready to give it a try? You have 5 minutes for Worksheet #3 Main Points.

Worksheet #3: Main Points

Speech Zero to Hero in One Hour from VirtualSpeechCoach.com

#1 Brainstorm at least 7 possible main points (2 min.)

Ask for each point: Does it support my purpose? Is it relevant to my audience?

#2 Narrow/combine your ideas into 2-3 main points, in order (3 min.)

Ask yourself: Is each point distinct? (not too much overlap), Are they in a logical order?

Example: (modified problem-solution organization, starting with benefits)
Main Point 1: Public speaking skills are important for engineers
Main Point 2: Public speaking can be challenging for engineers
Main Point 3: Opportunities to improve public speaking skills

Main Point 1:

Main Point 2:

Main Point 3 (Optional):

Step 4: Support points

Now you have come to the meat of your presentation, supporting your points.

A few common ways to support your points include:
- Anecdotal evidence: telling a story or offering a case study—make sure they are relevant!
- Empirical evidence: research and statistics
- Logical: reasoning based on facts
- Demonstration: show how something works

A useful approach that I use quite often is to combine anecdotal support (telling a story) with one other type of support. If your presentation ends up going longer than you anticipated, you can always cut out a point.

The next 3 pages, prior to worksheet #4, offer guidance in developing a relevant, engaging story for your speech. In some fields, a story could also be called a "case study" or "customer example."

Although there is space on the worksheet to indicate 2 subpoints for each main point, you may not want to have subpoints, if you don't have much clarity right now beyond your main point. If that is the case, just support your main point without having sub points.

You have 15 minutes to complete Worksheet #4: Support points

Pre-Worksheet Exercise: Engage Your Audience with Stories

Stories touch our emotions and linger in our minds. If you want your audience to remember your points, or you want to persuade, use stories. Facts tell, but stories sell. Use the following tips to create engaging stories:

1. **The story must be relevant to your point**. Don't tell a story just to tell a story.

2. **There must be conflict**. A story is usually only interesting if there is some sort of conflict (conflict types: person vs. person, person vs. self, person vs. nature, person vs. society, person vs. technology). Get to the conflict as quickly as possible. Provide just enough background/context to make the story relevant or understandable.

Here is the standard "Hero Story" format:

(Main character)_____ is in (circumstances/setting)_____ and needs to (Goal)_____ but faces _____(obstacles/opponents)

when_____ (Climax/conflict occurs, often more than once)

until _____ (resolution—obstacles or opponents are overcome)

3. **Use a little bit of drama**
   a) **The dramatic pause.** Pause a couple of seconds before and after a climatic situation or phrase to heighten the anticipation. "To be or not to be?" (pause, pause), "That is the question."
   b) **Dialogue.** Don't just narrate. Use narration to set up dialogue (characters talking to each other). Dialogue is the heart of an engaging story.
   c) **Act it out.** Let your facial expressions convey emotions. Get your body into the story. Don't just say, "We pushed the car out of the ditch," but actually act out at least the hand gesture of pushing.

Where can you get ideas for stories?

Your personal experiences. (should be the primary source for your stories). As related to your topic, what experiences have given you "aha" moments, moments that changed what you thought, felt, or did? Use photos, journals and other records to jog your memory.

Second-degree experiences. Second-degree experiences are ones in which someone told you about their experiences (lessons from your grandmother's life, a client's story or testimonial).

Other sources. You may have read or heard a story that is relevant to your presentation. If you use a story other than your own, you need to attribute the source.

Example: Tell Your Story

1. Know your point! What is the relevant point of the story? (*Example point: Champion the Underdog. My grandmother modeled for me how to stand up for people*)

2. Paint a picture (without dragging on, providing just enough detail to provide context) Example set up: *It was Christmas Eve, 1968. I was six years old and I still believed in Santa. We had just arrived at a family Christmas party--my mother's side of the family, all good Italian Catholics, with big families. Santa Claus was handing out gifts, calling out each child's name. . .*

3. Get them in the gut (What created feelings of Joy, Sadness, Fear, Anger or Frustration?)

4. Use a story structure (The points are indicated for the example story that follows):
    1. Main character: *6-year-old Diane*
    2. inciting event (a problem): *Diane didn't get a gift from Santa*
    3. What happened leading to the climax: *Grandma intervened*
    4. Climax/Turning point: *Santa gave Diane an awesome gift*
    5. Resolution/solution: *Diane learned an important lesson from Grandma*

As it got closer and closer to my turn, I squeezed my grandmother's hand. Finally, it was the last gift. My gift. Santa Claus raised it up high, and called out, "Ho, ho, ho, Theresa Coffee." (reaction) What?? I felt like I'd been sucker punched. Has that ever happened to you? Has someone else ever got something you deserved? Like a promotion or a job? Well that's how I felt. After I recovered from the shock, tears welled up and I looked up at my nana, my big Italian grandma, and said, "Santa forgot me!" My nana scooped me up in those fleshy arms, arms that every morning rolled out ravioli at an Italian restaurant, and said, "Oh no, Santa did not forget you!" And she passed me off to my parents who tried to shield me from what grandma was doing, but I saw her work the crowd and I saw her get her younger brothers, my great uncles, to work the crowd too. Well, a few minutes later, a sheepish-looking Santa Claus approached me. "Little Diane Williams, I'm sorry. Your gift was stuck at the bottom of my bag." And with a flourish, he pulled out a wad of bills. Fifty bucks! A small fortune to a six-year-old in 1968. My tears vanished, and I looked over at my nana. She was smiling like a Cheshire Cat. My grandmother taught me a couple of important lessons that day. The first was that it pays to have . . . mafia connections. Well it does pay to have influential people in your life. But the more important lesson was to be a champion for the underdog.

Exercise: Tell Your Story, Your Turn!

1. Know your point! What is the relevant point of the story?

2. Paint a picture (without dragging on, providing just enough detail to provide context)

3. Get them in the gut (What created feelings of Joy, Sadness, Fear, Anger or Frustration?)

(Relate to the audience's pain, if possible)

4. Use a story structure
   - Main character (can be a client or customer):

   - inciting event (a problem):

   - What happened leading to the climax:

   - Climax/Turning point:

   - Resolution/solution:

5. Practice and revise

Worksheet #4: Support Points

Speech Zero to Hero in One Hour from VirtualSpeechCoach.com

Common ways to support your points (can combine as time allows):
- Anecdotal: relevant story, case study, example, testimony/quote
- Empirical: research & statistics
- Logical: reasoning based on facts
- Demonstration: show how something works

Try this engaging approach for each point: anecdotal + one other type of support

Main Point 1:

Sub point:
    Support:
    Support:

Sub point:
    Support:
    Support:

Main Point 2:

Sub point:
    Support:
    Support:

Sub point:
    Support:
    Support:

Main Point 3 (optional):

Sub point:
    Support:
    Support:

Sub point:
    Support:
    Support:

Step 5: Open, Close

The opening and closing of your presentation are critical components, and the only parts I suggest memorizing.

You want to open in a way that gets the audience's attention, has them leaning forward with anticipation, and lets them know where you are going to take them.

Open with the 3 Ps, Pep, Promise, and Path:

- PEP—Get their attention with a thought-provoking question, a story, a relevant quote or a startling statistic.
- Promise—Specify the benefits to your audience
- Path—preview the points (or indicate how they will get the promise. For example, "Today you will learn how to use 3 tools").

For the conclusion you can reverse the 3 Ps

- Path-summarize points (review)
- Promise—Revisit the promise
- Pep—typically a call-to-action. What's the ONE next thing they can do?

If you have a Question & Answer session (Q&A)—end with a pre-planned statement.

You have 10 minutes to complete Worksheet #5: open, close.

Worksheet #5: Open, Close

Speech Zero to Hero in One Hour from VirtualSpeechCoach.com

3 Ps of a presentation introduction:

- Pep: get attention with question, story, quote, startling statistic, etc.
- Promise: specify benefits to audience
- Path: preview points (or indicate how they will get the promise, for example, "3 tools")

Open:

Pep:

Promise:

Path:

Close (essentially reverse the 3 Ps):

Path (summarize main points):

Promise (revisit the promise):

Pep (typically a call-to-action):

Note: if you have Q&A plan a second closing statement so that the ending is in your control. Don't just let your answer to the last random question be your close. Transition to a strong closing statement that you have pre-planned.

Step 6: Speech Notes

OK, if you are running out of time, you can simply take worksheet #4 and worksheet #5 and use them as your speech notes. However, I suggest that you condense your notes onto one page, which is what Worksheet #6 is for.

The first page of the worksheet is a speech notes example.

In the second page of the worksheet, make sure to write or type your notes so that you can easily read them at a glance. When I type my notes, I use font 14. Remember, you aren't typing out your entire speech, just the outline, or even just key words.

You have 5 minutes to complete Worksheet #6: Speech notes

Speech Notes Example

Note: This example is for a 30-45-minute presentation

Speech Zero to Hero in One Hour from VirtualSpeechCoach.com

<u>Speech Title:</u> Build a Better Engineering Career with Public Speaking

Open (P1-Pep, P2-Promise, P3-Path)

P1: Me as a young engineer ducking into restroom, P2: Developing public speaking skills will enhance your career, "today you will discover why" P3: state 3 points

Main Point 1: Public speaking skills are important for engineers

Sub point: Communication skills are critical for career advancement
Support: Research on executives valuing communications skills in employees
Support: Examples: project presentation, clarifying issues, interviewing, etc.

Sub point: Poor communication can lead to poor results (or disaster!)
Support: PMI study: Poor communication leads to project failure 1/3 of the time
Support: Challenger disaster (example)

Main Point 2: Public speaking can be challenging for engineers

Sub point: Engineers can overwhelm audiences with technical details
Support: Examples of overly technical PowerPoint
Support: Simple is better (evidence)

Sub point: Engineers can find it challenging to engage with the audience
Support: "Just the facts, Ma'am" approach is boring (research)
Support: Perfection is overrated (demonstration)

Main Point 3: Opportunities to improve public speaking skills

Sub point: opportunities to speak at work and conferences
Support: Ways to speak more at work (list)
Support: Ways to speak at conferences (list, example)

Sub point: opportunities to learn and practice public speaking skills
Support: Online and in-person classes, books
Support: Toastmasters (+ personal testimony)

Conclusion (P3-Path, P2-Promise, P1-Pep/call-to-action)

P3: review points, P2: you can greatly enhance your career, P1: Take advantage of the opportunities & take charge of your career development!

Worksheet #6: Speech Notes

Speech Zero to Hero in One Hour from VirtualSpeechCoach.com

Speech Title: _____

Open (P1-Pep, P2-Promise, P3-Path)

Main Point 1:

Sub point:
Support:
Support:

Sub point:
Support:
Support:

Main Point 2:

Sub point:
Support:
Support:

Sub point:
Support:
Support:

Main Point 3 (optional):

Sub point:
Support:
Support:

Sub point:
Support:
Support:

Conclusion (P3-Path, P2-Promise, P1-Pep/call-to-action)

Step 7: Focused Practice

There's not a worksheet for focused practice, but simply an approach. If you only have a few minutes to practice, then the opening and the closing are what you need to focus on so that you start well and end with impact.

First, take a moment to read through the delivery tips on the next page.

Second, rehearse your opening few sentences and closing few sentences (and if you say them slightly differently each time, that's OK).

If you have more than 5 minutes before "show time," spend more time rehearsing, which you can do in chunks of content if you don't have time to run through your entire presentation. I often practice in the car (I don't suggest doing so during rush hour traffic, however). Practice transitions from one part to the next. Practice telling any stories you are using. If you are using presentation slides, practice with them as well.

Top 10 Delivery Tips to Wow Your Audience

Speech Zero to Hero in One Hour from VirtualSpeechCoach.com

1. **Don't read.** Don't read your notes. Don't read your slides. Follow the rule "Talk to People Not to Paper." If you speak from an outline or brief keyword notes (in a large font), pause, stop speaking, mentally grab the next point, look up at the audience and then speak. When you read, you lose engaging eye contact with your audience.

2. **Speak conversationally,** unless the culture or setting require formal language.

3. **Smile,** especially at the start. It will relax you and warm up your audience.

4. **Memorize your opening and closing.** Start and finish strong. Memorizing your opening will give you a confident start.

5. **Pause.** Pause naturally, as in conversation. Pause before and after important or difficult words or concepts. Pause after rhetorical questions (even though you don't expect an answer after a rhetorical question, it gives the audience time to reflect).

6. **Don't cram your content!** Cut your content to comfortably fit the time and your audience's comprehension.

7. **Dress appropriately for your audience and the circumstances.** Wear something comfortable that you look good in (don't forget to wear clean, polished shoes in a business setting).

8. **Tell stories (or "case studies") that include a conflict or challenge.** Stories are concrete, connect with emotions, and are memorable. Facts tell, but stories sell.

9. **Focus on giving the audience a gift** (information, a new way of looking at something). It's not about you. It's about the audience.

10. **Let go of perfection.** Your audience won't typically realize if you said something differently than you planned. Or, even if you completely forget something. Just move on.

Bonus tip: Bring a bottle of water. There's nothing worse than having a tickle in your throat and seeing water in the back of the room. You can also take a sip to buy time to gather your thoughts.

How to Be a More Confident Speaker in 10 Seconds

You know your message. You know your audience. You've practiced at least a focused practice of the opening and close. Now, it's show-time! How can you bolster your self-confidence in the few seconds before you speak— even as you are walking up to deliver your opening lines?

I believe that your confidence level can be affected by changing how you act, how you feel and what you believe—in any order! The usual order is to work on your belief and then that will change how you feel which in turn will change how you act. You can reverse that order right before you speak. In the few seconds before you speak, you need to focus on action!

Here are 5 steps you can take in the 10 seconds before you open your mouth to speak. Steps 1-3 can be done while walking up to speak, or in combination with steps 4 and 5:

1. Breathe. Take a deep, calming breath. Remember your brain needs oxygen!

2. Stand tall. Good posture not only helps with your breath support while you speak, it also makes you look more confident. I use a "string theory" to quickly improve my posture right before I speak. I imagine a string being pulled from the ceiling that connects the top of my head to my chest to my pelvis. Try it right now! It even works when you are sitting.

3. Mentally rehearse your opening sentence or two. Your opening should be ready to charge out of the gate with power.

4. Eye Contact. Look at your audience for a second or two, with the attitude of "this is a gift I'm giving to you" and a pleasant expression. Connect with their eyes. A confident speaker looks into the eyes of his or her audience.

5. Smile. As you continue for a couple more seconds with eye contact and before you speak, turn your pleasant expression into a broad, warm smile, the genuine kind that crinkles your eyes. Of course, if your speech has a very serious start, you don't want to smile inappropriately, but a smile is a magnet to your audience.

And then, deliver your opening lines with confidence!

Easy PowerPoint Principles

If you are trying to create a presentation in an hour, you probably don't have time to create visuals in presentation creation tools such as PowerPoint. But, if you have a little extra time, presentation tools can enhance a presentation if used well. Create an elegant and simple PowerPoint by following these four easy tips:

1. **Plan outside of PowerPoint.** Don't start presentation planning in PowerPoint, but create a presentation that you could give without PowerPoint (especially useful if the technology fails), and then consider how you can enhance your presentation with the visual support of presentation software. Try planning on sticky notes that can be easily rearranged, and then transfer your sticky note outline to PowerPoint slides. Or, see the next page for a planning grid.

   Sticky note planning example:

2. **Use less text and more pictures/graphics.**
   Fewer words can help people understand more by reducing complexity. Personally, I try not to use more text or bullets than dictated by the 6X6 rule: No more than 6 bullets with no more than 6 words per bullet, with only 6 lines (no wrapping). Usually, I prefer much, much less text than even that. Pictures and simple graphical representation of data are easier to understand. And, if you don't have words on your slides, you can't read them!

3. **Use BIG pictures for a BIG impact** (let the picture take up the whole slide, if possible)

4. **Proof-read and then practice your presentation several times** (don't read the slides!). Have a hard-copy outline to keep you on track, especially if the technology fails.

   For an 8-minute video of PowerPoint tips: http://bit.ly/ezppt

Plan your PowerPoint

Using your outline, consider how you could visually support your presentation. Use the boxes below or sticky notes:

Free Online Course

Take the free companion course that guides you through the 7-step speech development approach in this book (with short intro videos). The course also allows you to download the worksheets:

http://bit.ly/speechhero

Second Set of Worksheets

A second set of the 6 worksheets, the focused practice approach, and 10 Delivery Tips follow. These can be used with the free online course, or for a second speech.

Worksheet #1: The 2 "Knows"

Speech Zero to Hero in One Hour from VirtualSpeechCoach.com

Understanding a couple of critical considerations before you start creating your presentation will save you time and frustration later!

#1 Know the Requirements

Date:
Time:
Location:
Length of presentation:
Topic:
What you are expected to bring (e.g. handout/report/introduction):

Other:

#2 Know Your Audience

Audience composition (executives, peers, customers, etc.):

Is there a segment of the audience of primary importance?

What level of knowledge about my topic does the audience have?

What are the audience pain points, as related to your topic?
     Pain point 1:
     Pain point 2:
     Pain point 3:

Why would the audience care about your topic?

What do you want the audience to think, feel, and/or do?
Think:
Feel:
Do (do you have a call-to-action?):

Worksheet #2: Big Picture

Speech Zero to Hero in One Hour from VirtualSpeechCoach.com

Start with your purpose and decide on your organizational structure to support that purpose.

#1 Select ONE Specific Purpose (keeping in mind your audience)

Step 1: What is the main general purpose of your presentation? Circle one:
To inform, to persuade, to entertain

Step 2: What is your specific purpose? (start your statement with your general purpose and phrase it to include a benefit for the audience)

Example: *To persuade engineers that developing public speaking skills will enhance their careers.* (the benefit is "enhance their careers")

> **Your specific purpose:**

#2 Decide on an organization structure to communicate your main idea

- Topical: Most common presentation structure, arranges information into subtopics

- Binary: Problem-Solution, Cause-Effect, Compare-Contrast, Advantages-Disadvantages

- Sequential: Chronological, Demonstration (step 1, step 2, step 3)

- Spatial (parts relating to a whole, geographical)

> **Your presentation structure:**
>
> **Speech Title:**

Worksheet #3: Main Points

Speech Zero to Hero in One Hour from VirtualSpeechCoach.com

#1 Brainstorm at least 7 possible main points (2 min.)

Ask for each point: Does it support my purpose? Is it relevant to my audience?

#2 Narrow/combine your ideas into 2-3 main points, in order (3 min.)

Ask yourself: Is each point distinct? (not too much overlap), Are they in a logical order?

Example: (modified problem-solution organization, starting with benefits)
Main Point 1: Public speaking skills are important for engineers
Main Point 2: Public speaking can be challenging for engineers
Main Point 3: Opportunities to improve public speaking skills

Main Point 1:

Main Point 2:

Main Point 3 (Optional):

Worksheet #4: Support Points

Speech Zero to Hero in One Hour from VirtualSpeechCoach.com

Common ways to support your points (can combine as time allows):
- Anecdotal: relevant story, case study, example, testimony/quote
- Empirical: research & statistics
- Logical: reasoning based on facts
- Demonstration: show how something works

Try this engaging approach for each point: anecdotal + one other type of support

Main Point 1:

Sub point:
    Support:
    Support:

Sub point:
    Support:
    Support:

Main Point 2:

Sub point:
    Support:
    Support:

Sub point:
    Support:
    Support:

Main Point 3 (optional):

Sub point:
    Support:
    Support:

Sub point:
    Support:
    Support:

Worksheet #5: Open, Close

Speech Zero to Hero in One Hour from VirtualSpeechCoach.com

3 Ps of a presentation introduction:

- Pep: get attention with question, story, quote, startling statistic, etc.
- Promise: specify benefits to audience
- Path: preview points (or indicate how they will get the promise, for example, "3 tools")

Open:

Pep:

Promise:

Path:

Close (essentially reverse the 3 Ps):

Path (summarize main points):

Promise (revisit the promise):

Pep (typically a call-to-action):

Note: if you have Q&A, plan a second closing statement so that the ending is in your control. Don't just let your answer to the last random question be your close. Transition to a strong closing statement that you have pre-planned.

Worksheet #6: Speech Notes

Speech Zero to Hero in One Hour from VirtualSpeechCoach.com

Speech Title: _____

Open (P1-Pep, P2-Promise, P3-Path)

Main Point 1:

> **Sub point:**
> Support:
> Support:
>
> **Sub point:**
> Support:
> Support:

Main Point 2:

> **Sub point:**
> Support:
> Support:
>
> **Sub point:**
> Support:
> Support:

Main Point 3 (optional):

> **Sub point:**
> Support:
> Support:
>
> **Sub point:**
> Support:
> Support:

Conclusion (P3-Path, P2-Promise, P1-Pep/call-to-action)

Step 7: Focused Practice

There's not a worksheet for focused practice, but simply an approach. If you only have a few minutes to practice, then the opening and the closing are what you need to focus on so that you start well and end with impact.

First, take a moment to read through the delivery tips again, on the next page.

Second, rehearse your opening few sentences and closing few sentences (and if you say them slightly differently each time, that's OK).

If you have more than 5 minutes before "show time," spend more time rehearsing, which you can do in chunks of content if you don't have time to run through your entire presentation. I often practice in the car (I don't suggest doing so during rush hour traffic, however). Practice transitions from one part to the next. Practice telling any stories you are using. If you are using presentation slides, practice with them as well.

Top 10 Delivery Tips to Wow Your Audience

Speech Zero to Hero in One Hour from VirtualSpeechCoach.com

1. **Don't read.** Don't read your notes. Don't read your slides. Follow the rule "Talk to People Not to Paper." If you speak from an outline or brief keyword notes (in a large font), pause, stop speaking, mentally grab the next point, look up at the audience and then speak. When you read, you lose engaging eye contact with your audience.

2. **Speak conversationally,** unless culture or setting requires formal language.

3. **Smile,** especially at the start. It will relax you and warm up your audience.

4. **Memorize your opening and closing.** Start and finish strong. Memorizing your opening will give you a confident start.

5. **Pause.** Pause naturally, as in conversation. Pause before and after important or difficult words or concepts. Pause after rhetorical questions (even though you don't expect an answer after a rhetorical question, it gives the audience time to reflect).

6. **Don't cram your content!** Cut your content to comfortably fit the time and your audience's comprehension.

7. **Dress appropriately for your audience and the circumstances.** Wear something comfortable that you look good in (don't forget to wear clean, polished shoes in a business setting).

8. **Tell stories (or "case studies") that include a conflict or challenge.** Stories are concrete, connect with emotions, and are memorable. Facts tell, but stories sell.

9. **Focus on giving the audience a gift** (information, a new way of looking at something). It's not about you. It's about the audience.

10. **Let go of perfection.** Your audience won't typically realize if you said something differently than you planned. Or, even if you completely forget something. Just move on.

Bonus tip: Bring a bottle of water. There's nothing worse than having a tickle in your throat and seeing water in the back of the room. You can also take a sip to buy time to gather your thoughts.

About the Author

 Diane Windingland is the author of several books on communication skills including *Cat Got Your Tongue?, 12 Ways to be a Confident Speaker, Public Speaking Lessons from TED Talks* and more. Originally trained as an engineer, she trains and coaches subject matter experts to present with clarity and confidence, shaping what they know into presentations that engage and get results.

As a member of Toastmasters International, she has achieved the organization's highest educational award for public speaking and leadership, Distinguished Toastmaster.

Diane recommends joining a Toastmaster club as a cost-effective and fun way to develop communication and leadership skills in a peer-led environment. Go to toastmasters.org for more information or to find a club.

When Diane isn't busy speaking, writing, developing courses, or coaching, she enjoys traveling with her husband, spending time with family, cooking healthy meals, and helping people become the best versions of themselves.

Bring Diane to your organization and help people become the best versions of themselves as they learn how to create and deliver presentations that are clear and engaging.

Diane's website: VirtualSpeechCoach.com

Contact Diane:

Diane@VirtualSpeechCoach.com

612-306-4214